Soul in a Shell

Soul in a Shell

Dylan Byall

Copyright © 2025 Dylan Byall

All rights reserved.
No part of this book may be reproduced, stored in a retrieval system, or transmitted in any form or by any means, electronic and mechanical, including photocopying and recording, or by any information storage and retrieval system, or be used to train generative artificial intelligence (AI) technologies or develop machine-learning language models, without the prior written permission of the publisher, except in the case of brief quotations used in reviews, articles, or scholarly work.

ISBN: 979-8-9987444-1-9

First Edition

Printed in the United States of America
The text of this book is set in Minion Pro

This is a work of creative nonfiction. The poems and prose are inspired by personal experience and memory. Some details have been altered or imagined for literary effect. The views expressed are solely those of the author and do not represent the official policies or positions of the U.S. Navy, the Department of Defense, or any agency of the U.S. government.

To learn more about the author and future publications, visit:
Instagram: @dylanbyallwriter

Cover design by Nicholas Kempton
Illustrations by Nicholas Kempton
Interior layout by Iram Allam
Art contributions by Francesca Possati
Author photo by Matt Mendelsohn
Editing by Martha Sprackland and Edward Wall

For Chasity

Contents

Introduction   1

An old Turkish proverb goes   3
I look at my phone and the world, spinning like a bullet, slows   6

I. ALT   9

Crossroads   11
Trails   12
The man had many masks   14
Catch-22   17
Bull   18
Declaration   19
roach   20
Zoo   21
The Fukuoka Supreme Store & The Fall of Rome   23
The Megalopolis   25
Community Service   26
They say a rolling stone gathers no moss, but all rolling ever did was grind me down   27
A Fire Station for Sorrow   28
Ghost Stories   30
Giving Up the Ghost   32
The Infinite Scroll   34
Virginia Beach   36
Portrait in Red   38
Portrait in Blue   39
Smile Hotel Sasebo   40
Field Manual: Light Duty (Erasure)   41
In This Industrial Home   42

II. CTRL — 45

Shell (noun) — 47
Shell Program (noun) — 48
Mouth — 49
Panic — 51
On High Alert (2021-2025) — 53
On June 18, 2023 — 55
United States — 56
Investigator (2023) — 58
A Heart Like a Barrel of Oil — 60
CTRL — 62
I see myself, an old man, self-admitted to a bar — 64
The Wax Candle / Its Source Code — 66
Champs D'Honneur (Erasure) — 69
I cheated on hope, — 70
Frankenstein's Monster — 71
Christmas, 1914 — 72

III. ESC — 75

Even in war zones — 77
Metamorphosis — 78
Dear Texan Wife — 79
The Good Life (Erasure) — 80
O, Japan — 81
My early life was a war — 82
Setsubun — 83
Sister, — 85
April (Erasure) — 87
April 15th — 88
Breakfast After the Titanic Sank — 89
Vending Machine — 91
A Taxi Drive in Sasebo — 92
Prospecting — 93
Philippines Sea Storm — 94
The Banana Tree — 95

What the Mountain Birds Know	96
In His Eyes	97
The thing about falling is	98
Sobriety	99
Dropping the Ball	101
If King Henry VIII had remained faithful to his first wife, or loved his subjects, would he have died a broken soul, suffering from obesity?	102
Tom and Jerry	103
The baby-blue robin eggs	104
Sunset	105
Sunday Night in Tokyo	106
At the hospital exit	107
In the Silver Chalice	108

IV. FN 109

Soul (noun)	111
Family Matter	112
Humanity	115
Coming into Our Own	116
The Golden Spiral	117
Homecoming	120
Cautious Love	121
Pariah	122
6 a.m., driving to Portsmouth Naval Hospital, I notice a traffic jam.	123
Lightning	128
Vineyard	129
With sincerity,	131
Smile Hotel Sasebo II	132
Celebrate!	134
Love of my Life,	136
In the morning	137
Sunlight on the turning tides,	138
When we first met,	140
Notes & Acknowledgements	141

Spring passes and one remembers one's innocence.
Summer passes and one remembers one's exuberance.
Autumn passes and one remembers one's reverence.
Winter passes and one remembers one's perseverance.

—Yoko Ono

Introduction

Edward O. Wilson once said, "The real problem with humanity is the following: We have Paleolithic emotions, medieval institutions, and godlike technology. And it is terrifically dangerous, and it is now approaching a point of crisis overall."

That quote struck me like a lightning bolt when I found it a few days ago. To my surprise, Wilson said this in 2009 during a discussion featured in Harvard Magazine. It encapsulates so much of what I've tried to explore in this book—and its sequel "Ad Disastra", which I'm already writing.

My approach to poetry, and writing in general, has always been rooted in observation. I enjoy watching the world carefully. As a teenager, I fell in love with writers who documented their time and gave voice to the overlooked—Gertrude Stein, John Steinbeck, F. Scott Fitzgerald, and Ernest Hemingway. I admired how they captured the spirit and struggles of their eras. That same urge—to speak to the now—led me to set aside the novel I was working on and turn to poetry.

In 2020, at the start of the COVID-19 pandemic, I was stationed in Japan, which is, after all, said to be the cultural crossroads of the modern world. I had too much to say during this time and didn't believe it could all be best said in a novel. Poetry gave me a way to say more with less—to distill the chaos into something contained. I thought it would take a year. It took five.

I encountered Wilson's quote in a Facebook post. Ironic, given how often Facebook appears in a handful of these poems as both a drug and a tool of surveillance. His quote didn't just appear in my feed by chance. I suspect the algorithm read my Google Docs, my searches, and knew from other interactions what I cared about.

And yet, here I am—writing this introduction, sure to return to Facebook soon after and accept the next IOS update without reading the terms and conditions. I speak out against the systems that control us, even as I pass through their corridors every day. Like many, I carry the quiet ache of knowing I am a cog in the very machine which I fear.

But still, there's hope.

Ideas can move mountains. Seeds can grow trees strong enough to crack concrete. With these poems, I want to plant seeds that give strength and bear fruit for the trees—not the axe. Especially not the axe that wants to fool us that it's a tree just because its handle is made of wood.

So, I keep writing. Scattering words and ideas like Johnny Appleseed, the folk hero my dad told me stories about when I was young. Living still like Old Dan Tucker, who, as the old rhyme goes, "was a mighty man who washed his face in a frying pan."

No matter how much money is in my hands, I write to remember, I write to resist. I write because some things need to be said—and felt. Even as godlike technology and medieval institutions try to cheapen the soul, I express these Paleolithic emotions for the trees to always remember their value in this chaotic contemporary world.

An old Turkish proverb goes

the forest was shrinking
but the trees kept voting for the axe;
for the axe was clever
and convinced the trees
that because his handle
was made of wood,
he was one of them.

The trees
and the axe
both saw change
as pure-hearted ambition.

Most of my life, I've been a sapling.
I've raised my hands in the axe's name—
voted for its wooden grip,
not knowing it would chop mine off.

The world spins faster than I can hold on to,
strapped six inches from a screen,
staring six feet into my grave.

This tiny world controls too much:
in endless circles
the microchip reflects its twin—
a snake eating its tail for infinity.

I scroll past my reflection—
pixelated, fragmented,
a mosaic of who I was
and who I've become.

The divine Tree of Life withers
as we lose ourselves, pixel by pixel.
I open my mouth to speak,
but every word is erased.
Every thought censored.
Every scream silenced.

And yet—
there are moments of clarity,
rebellion chanting in the noise,
the possibility of love and survival
against systems grinding us
to ash and static.

And there's me again;
me, a boy made of pine
who wanted to be real.
Playing video games in his underwear,
feeling like Superman,
as though winning one more level
would mean saving something—
or somebody who needed it.

The controller felt right in my palms,
like a shield against a world
I didn't understand.

I never thought I'd grow up
just to hand it to someone else.
But here I am—
wondering if the forest within the screen
is worth saving,
or if it's already lost.

And then I remember:
the axe is not the forest.

The screen is not the world.
Somewhere, beneath the static,
a seed still grows—

for us.
For whatever still grows.

Not for the axe,
but for the trees.

I look at my phone and the world, spinning like a bullet, slows

Facebook asks me, *What's on your mind?*
I type, then hit post on:

> *I'm going to tell you the whole story—the truth, the good parts, the bad, the nasty parts, the fantastic, the straight-up dirty, and the ones too salacious to even read about in the news. The truth is, you've been lied to.*

Before it pops up,
I get the message:
Your post is against our community standards—
and just like that, it's removed.

I feel mute.
My emotions are a nuclear family
and its atom split.

All I can think is,

"You're such a ▮▮"

I imagine the moderators screaming back:
"No, you are! You rat piece of ▮▮"
But they don't have a face.

The next week, I'm in a debate online,
ensnared by rage-bait.
Someone responds with 💀 💀 💀
I don't know what to say.
Someone else adds 💀 💀 💀 💀

I finally respond, though it tumbles out as █████████
█████

Before I know it,
there's an army of omens
surrounding my words.

And suddenly,

I'm rising from a 🪦
I never knew I slept in.

I. ALT

Some of us think holding on makes us strong; but sometimes it is letting go.

—Hermann Hesse

Crossroads

<u>The bottom line is:</u>
I signed it all away
for a shot at living
at full capacity

without us.

Trails

Clear blue autumn skies.
Contrails slash, turn gray, then grow—
Forecast fails, rain falls.

Jet streams lace the air,
Flow through rivers, ice caps, seas—
In each breath we breathe.

* * *

I press the button
On the break room's ice machine,
Holding hot coffee.

My lips are burnt raw.
I dab them with wet ice, then
The news runs again.

"Well! I've often seen a cat without a grin," thought Alice; "but a grin without a cat! It's the most curious thing I ever saw in all my life!"

> —Lewis Carroll, *Alice's Adventures in Wonderland*

The man had many masks;

his world offered him many more.

He wore a neatly pressed khaki Navy Service Uniform,
lines on both sides of his chest, a ribbon rack with five rows;
stars shining like the North Star.
I approached him in the far corner of the cafeteria during lunch.
He looked up with big, red eyes, toying with a Navy-brand pen.
He jittered—I initially suspected from PTSD,
then I saw the empty can of Red Bull in front of him.
He shook my hand and said he needed to pack his booth soon,
but had a few minutes to talk.

I'd rehearsed my words for days,
but as I spoke, they fell from my mouth like lead.
"I want to enlist," I said. "Do you know who to talk to?"

He chuckled. "You're talking to him. I'm the person to talk to."

"Oh." I felt my face flush, then breathed and steadied my gaze.
"I want to join the Navy by the end of the summer. Can I?"

He glanced at his wristwatch, counting time.
"How old are you?"

"Eighteen," I said.

"Good," he raised his gray eyebrows.
"You won't need your parents' permission."

He looked around as if a list of qualifications floated in the air.
"What are you now? A junior? Senior?"

"I'm a senior."

"Planning to graduate?"

"Yes, for sure."

"Good. You need a diploma. Have you taken the ASVAB?"

"I've heard of it. But no, I haven't taken it."

"It's like the SAT," he said, clicking his pen on the plastic tabletop.
"Just a military aptitude test. It's easy."
He checked his watch again.
He handed me a pamphlet illustrating the benefits of joining.
I flipped it over and saw his name and number on the back.

Little did I know, I was looking down a rabbit hole.
I would dive down it,
landing at the end of another decade of my life.

As he stood, his wristwatch sparkled silver
bright enough to lure ravens.

Looking back now, he must have believed he was talking to a crow,
hungry for shiny objects and glory.
And maybe I was. Maybe I was both Alice and a crow.
I was willing to fight a Jabberwocky,
addicted to the silver spoon I never had.

He shook my hand firmly, vertical—perfectly balanced,
as if to say he was my friend, and this was an equal transaction.
He smiled a knowing smile,
the kind that said he'd seen it all before,
but still believed in the power of new beginnings.

My papers were finalized on November 5, 2016.
I left home on July 25, 2017.

Catch-22

When I was a teenager, I read a classic
about the absurdity of armed conflict,
set in the middle of World War II.

What astounded me was how
officers censored soldiers' letters home,
never imagining that in our digital peacetime
██████ still silences us every day.

Bull

My horns thrust out,
two sharpened lances,
my hooves,

hard as steel,
scattering dirt into the air
like a trencher's spinning blades.

Then life,
with a sudden, sharp snap,
whips across my face,
leaving its red handprint
seared into my skin.

The crowd roars.

I stand frozen
and wonder why
I ever charged at all.

Declaration

We stand there, "manning the rails,"
a paper-doll chain ornamenting the edges of our flight deck.
Yokosuka's morning sun climbs over the mountains cradling
    the bay.
Stripes of red light cut across our watering eyes.
We stand still with our hands folded on the small of our backs.
Our thumbs cross & our feet are spread a distance apart.
This is called "parade rest."
It tells outsiders, "We've completed our mission & now
we're back on shore, invigorated as the day we left."

One bullet could shred our paper bodies.

But you know what they say:
The pen is mightier than the sword.

roach

you're under
its thumb—
but you need
the thumb
to shield you
from the boot.

you use your might
to hold the thumb
until you have
opportunity
to escape.

Zoo

In their cameras,
high on the Flight Deck,
we became smelly apes, bored in an exhibit,
waving big sticks around.

Our M6s slung over our shoulders,
we took confident strides along the ship's edge,
looking onto the public 118 feet below
parking their bikes and cars
to catch glimpses of us.

Many of the Japanese watched us
with intense, untrusting stares
as if we ourselves discovered fire,
burnt them once with it, and now came
scraping another match along the flint pier.

Some took pictures of us
like we were exotic animals
they had seen on Animal Planet.
A few were careful, like archaeologists
while restoring elusive artifacts
fresh from the dig.

*Our military's history
is revered by some,
and denounced by others.*

That night in Iwakuni Harbor,
the locals turned their cameras on us
like ghost-hunters chasing orbs,
hoping to catch spirits
before they vanished into purgatory.

Some clicked defiantly,
like visitors warned not to photograph
a cursed relic in an occult museum,
unafraid of the stories.
Others looked worried,
as if they'd captured a demon
in their frames.

When they returned the next morning,
lining their bulky cars by the rails,
we dropped our mooring lines
and vanished into the horizon
faster than a Polaroid develops.

When I was a teenager,
a man named Terry Thompson
took his life after unleashing
fifty exotic animals
into Zanesville, Ohio.
My family and I were driving
out of Newark after antique shopping
when we heard the news on the radio.
In the dark forest, my mom swore
she saw the reflective eyes of
a leopard staring back.
The trees closed in on either side
as the moon hid beneath
a blanket of cloud.

Now, I feel like I'm part of
Uncle Sam's private collection,
and he's suicidal.

He's just freed me into a new world,
where I'm authorized to be shot on sight
or shipped off
to another zoo.

The Fukuoka Supreme Store
& The Fall of Rome

October, 2023, I had two months left in Japan. I decided to drift—my soul, wanting to map this place in memory—my body, wanting to plant its flag one last time.

I got a room at the Tenjin in Fukuoka for forty dollars. I keyed in, dropped off my bookbag, then headed out. As the sun descended, cutting across tall buildings, I walked alone, at peace in the orange light of the shopping district.

I found myself joining the back of the long, colorfully dressed line in a well-lit alley. I waited twenty minutes until I stepped into the Supreme store for the first time. Never worn their brand, never understood the hype.

The air smelled faintly of a candle, and I stood on a waxed wooden floor as clean as a for-sale studio flat. A TV blared '90s-style commercials, surrounded by a collage of stills that flickered like channel-surfing: a mouth with teeth bared and bleeding gums, then a shot of Marilyn Monroe, and a close-up of a honeybee caught mid-pollination on a tulip. Screens staring out into endless eyes. Eyes that stared back.

A burly porcelain figure greeted us at the entrance. Marker-drawn smile, a red Supreme-patterned sash around his neck. His body bent forward in a bow—he was a Shintō monk, and this was his dōjō. The shelves were nearly bare, stocked like a minimalist's closet. Two items of each design, just enough to whisper scarcity. Just enough to provoke desire. One T-shirt had a gas station glowing neon red against the night. A sign hung above: "Hell."

Another shirt displayed the cover of *American Psycho*, Patrick Bateman's face split by a skinless smile. Yet another bore a heatmap of the United States in infrared shades, with a scale at the bottom labeling the colors "Shit," "Shit," "Shit," "Shit."

Japanese shoppers clustered around that one, murmuring in low voices. I wondered if that's how the world saw us—bright and burning, but still just shades of shit. I saw it the same way.

I wasn't working for passion, just a paycheck. I'd been doing it ever since I realized the news didn't tell the news. It hadn't since I was born. I'd learned that at Great Grandpa Byall's house with Fox News echoing through the walls. I'd learned it again at Grandma Sherry's place, where CNN blared its own echoes.

Some people see the U.S. as a dignitary trying to play leader. But in 2023, I imagined it as Maximus Aurelius entering the colosseum, wounded beneath its armor. Even though it knew the wound was there, it knew it had to fight. And even though it might collapse on the world stage, it would still step into the arena—because that's what empires do.

Standing in that Supreme store, I felt the pulse of something decaying beneath the surface, something true, hidden under the brand's glossy sheen. Maybe that's what made it Supreme, made America supreme. Maybe that's what makes us all.

Something waiting to fight, even when it could already be lost.

The Megalopolis

Acid rain lashes streets.
Beyond the city's border,
Crabs hide in charred shells.

Community Service

Plastic mountains grow,
Landfills drowning in a sea—
Clean-up crews—Christ! Ants!

They say a rolling stone gathers no moss, but all rolling ever did was grind me down

We work so long,
moving with
or against the wind,
forgetting that
time will erode even our statues
and return us
to the cradling arms of the ocean.

These days, much like the ocean,
I'm looking up at the skies,
searching for a glimpse of you.

A Fire Station for Sorrow

where I could set it down
gently on the doorstep
and leave it for good.
I wish there were a suction hose
to draw up this sadness,
to wash it away.

* * *

Shellbacks wake us at 4 a.m.
banging trashcan-lid cymbals,
blowing on whistles,
spraying water hoses.

We hit the Flight Deck after 5.

I've heard sea stories
where, during the ceremony,
the fake priest would baptize
in AFFF firefighting foam.

We pass the Equator.

Years later,
because it runs off
into the water system,
a vivid premonition shows me
stage 3 cancer rearing its slick head.

I reclaim my sorrow,
an orphan, adopted,
but I never truly left.

Watch—

      how quickly,
on the muster sheet
smelling of fresh ink
and still warm paper,
you cross the line
through ~~my name~~.

Ghost Stories

When I first arrived aboard the *Reagan*, they whispered tales—
of security Nightwatch, the hours after midnight,
patrolling the silent superstructure in pairs.
Voices echoing through hollow passageways,
yet when they turned the corner, no one was there.

They said a carrier onboard delivery had gone awry,
the plane missed its mark, plunged into the ocean.
Three of eleven lost to the relentless tide
just a month before I arrived.

Less than a year later, another sailor,
on liberty in Guam,
was swallowed by the sea.

Too many murmurs,
too few moments of silence.

That's when I understood—
every ghost story in the Navy
is the echo of past tragedy.

We grew up in an America
that lifted us high,
called us *heroes*.

But we never imagined
we could become Macbeth—
heroes, tragically slain
by the ambitions of a nation,
as if glory could outweigh
the cost of the crown.

The crowned Eagle lifting us in battle,
only to leave us
homeless in the streets by the thousands
when the fighting is done.

While we cut hair
in the crew barbershop,
a marine once joked to me:
"Marines learn how to live in tents
because when we get out,
we already know how to live in one."

I paused, clippers in hand, and thought—
even in death, their ghosts
must carry their rucksacks forever
just as we never let go of our seabags.

Giving Up the Ghost

I thought heaven was in a computer.
Dad's soul was already gone
when the green light flashed on.
We used to pray to God at dinner.
Our food, our thoughts, our vitality,
now sacrificed to fiery phone screens
before our plates are scrubbed
by the dishwasher's plastic hands.

Mom, Dad, and I sit on the couch—
our first coffin,
the shell we crawl into
when the outside world is too hot.
And it's only getting warmer.
At night our eyes
shine in the dark room,
empty, white as dry-erase boards.

A part of us dies
when it shuts off after
asking if we're still watching.

Are you still watching?
In our trance,
we forget how to respond.

So the machine gives up its ghost
to the internal purgatory where
we confuse dying with living.

And our ghosts
sulk in the cold shell of the house.

* * *

Playing charades,
I reach into the bowl
and pull out a paper, reading:

Fisherman

My hands gesture reeling in a fish.

It feels so much like the actual thing—
just going through the motions of it.

And I wonder
between their wrong guesses,

Are you still watching?

The Infinite Scroll

Once upon a time—
Click
Reports are telling us a cat is stuck in a tree on Elm Street.
Click
Brad sent you a friend request
Click
They're bringing out the ladder. Aw—look at her! She's so scared and high up there!
Click
Hi sweetie, I miss you. Look. I have some bad news. Your grandpa's just d—
Click
Pew, pew, pew
Bloody murder
Click
In a faraway land there was a knight—
Click
Netflix
Click
Hulu. HBO Max
Click
Who rescued a princess and they fell in love—
Click
Facebook
Scroll, scroll, scroll, scroll
Like, like, like
Click
And they lived happily ever after.
Click
Listen, I've been trying to reach—
Click
Grubhub

Scroll, scroll
Select
Choose your tip amount
$0.00
Your order is confirmed
Knock, knock
Ring, ring
Click
Hey, Grandpa would really appreciate it if you—
Click
The cat has been saved and is unharmed!
Like
TikTok
Scroll, scroll, scroll, scroll, scroll
Like, like, like, like, like
Scroll, scroll, scroll
Tik tok, tik tok
Scroll, scroll
Tik tok
Click

Virginia Beach

Before I flew in, I saw on Apple News
someone took a long drive off a short pier.
Fear hit me like shrapnel, and I thought,
What a long way I've come in such a short time.
But how long can I keep living like this?

Will I burn out or bleed out first?

It's a question for our contemporary culture—
evolving sideways, always reinventing standards,
uninstalling and reinstalling the wheel,
pushing the envelope
until snail mail is a foreign concept.

Burnout culture is burning through
every match in its matchbox,
and the darkness is closing in.

Scars run as deep as the Mariana Trench.
They scream through picket signs
and cry in graffiti.

Waves come and go.

We sit on Virginia Beach, looking
out from our rented, overpriced cabana—
the same size as our Chapel Lake apartment,
so you know it feels right at home.
The colors melt on the horizon,
a red, white, and blue Bomb Pop
licked by a parched tongue.
When we pack up,
they seem to break apart.

Waves come in farther.

I've never heard
of a mass shooting in the ocean.

I wish this land would heal itself
and declare itself sacred ground,
so no more blood is shed,
these footprints, smoothed over.

Portrait in Red

Today, May 14, 2024,
King Charles unveiled himself,
painted by Jonathon Yeo.
A stark departure from the royal portraiture
I'd seen in textbooks as a kid
and on Google as an adult.
Mixed reviews poured in—
from critics, netizens alike.

The most popular comment on Instagram:
"Looks like he's in hell."
Another posted,
"It looks like he's bathing in blood."

Yeo paints Charles's face with realism:
textures of age, tones of power.
The rest dissolves into a slurry of red paint,
a sword rising from the depths,
gripped in both hands.
A butterfly hovers near his shoulder—
some claim it's Queen Elizabeth's spirit,
while he called it a symbol of his ascent
among other meanings.

It terrified me.
Maybe it's a sign of the times,
a testament to how we now frame
the elite.

In these times,
they say a social contract
feels like a deal with the Devil.
But I know every deal breeds a devil of its own.

Portrait in Blue

When I was a kid, for years
I was hostage to a nightmare,
until I strangled it into a dream.
Grown now, it tortures me,
forced to free myself from failure's grip.

Unveiled, I sit in my blue-lit silence,
deconstructing my life, other people's lives,
and these frames we got so used to
you could almost call them family portraits.

I look at these ivory hands,
once so innocent, now slathered in thick red.

The butterfly, disgusted—beats on, flying
where freedom isn't just a word,
but a place.

Smile Hotel Sasebo

I'm reminded of a Super 8:
>   a bed,
>   cheap, clean, hard as a brick,
>   the pungent smell
>   of ten thousand cigarettes
>   pressed to one thousand lips,
>   and the curtains,
>   faded, paper-thin.

There's a man yelling in the other room.
>   *I don't know why.*

There's a woman yelling back.
>   *I don't know why.*

Someone opens a window in another room.
The wind howls through the walls.
>   *I don't know why.*

There's a party in the farthest room—
laughter spills under the door,
so close I could touch it,
yet I don't lift a finger.
>   *I don't know why.*

I'm in this room alone,

>   *and I don't know why.*

The silence drives its heel into my heart,
heavier than all of this noise.

>   *I wish I didn't know why.*

But I do.

Field Manual: Light Duty (Erasure)
after Kevin Powers

Think   of
                                    the burned man's
                                        pain
                                    end it,
                    loud.   scream.
                        Call this "relief."

                            rest,
the .22 into your palm

                                for a TV crew.

the unending
            often it becomes absurd.
Think
        skinny ribs.
Think   grief

In This Industrial Home

I fade into thin air
like sparks from a chain.
It drives you there,
this pain,
it drives you into
showers of champagne,
a steady flow
of vomit down the drain,
liquor bottles
pouring their relentless rain,
pushing you off a cliff.
Now you can't
remember your name.
I'm drowning
in this life's Great Flood of shame.

That's what it does to you.
The industrial work environment,
the industrial home,
the industrial thoughts.
That's what it does to you—
the industrial bed, six feet long, two feet high,
the incessant drilling of power saws,
the sleepless nights.
It's what it does to you,
the strips of bars a ten-minute walk away,
the only businesses that thrive here,
roaches festering in fallout.
That's what it does to you—
Pleasure Island.
The aftermath of alcoholism.
It's what it does to you.

Livestock that thinks of itself as farmers.
That's what it does to you—
the denial:
neverending flames
we mere mortals
are commanded to tame.
I promise,
you won't be the same.

II. CTRL

Horror fiction shows us that the control we believe we have is purely illusory, and that every moment we teeter on chaos and oblivion.

—Clive Barker

Shell (noun)
/SHel/

1. the hard protective outer case of a mollusk or crustacean
2. an explosive artillery projectile or bomb
3. short for <u>shell program</u>

Shell Program (noun)
/'SHel ˌprōgram/

1. a program which provides an interface between the user and the operating system
2. a program which allows the user to use the operating system

Mouth

Overworked, weary,
I let the car guide me home.
Headlights blur with smog.

The dirt trail vanishes
like squid ink swirling through twilight;
this home, a dark void.

The remote sings its song.
The TV flickers with whispers:
"Come here, come closer."

"Come to me—come, come."
My legs move like marionettes,
unstuck from the couch.

The peppered static clears.
Silhouettes shift behind the screen—
I reach out, trembling.

Nothing. Hard glass, echoes.
The next night, something found my hand—
its touch burned like ice.

"Don't be scared, look. Here."
The screen opened its mouth wide.
I stared, breathless—trapped.

Bright light, endless white.
Someplace like purgatory
hummed inside of it.

The static swallows me whole,
its signal drills into my mind—
now I hum its tune.

I walk down the street,
heading to the office again.
My eyes are hollow glass.

Panic

When COVID clutched the States
in its iron grip
I saw on Facebook
that toilet paper
was the first thing to go.

The future, a foot away in all its ugly glory,
flashed across worldwide screens, screaming,
You're gonna shit your pants when you see this!

On a weekday, Yokosuka Naval Base shut down.
"Leave and you'll be prosecuted,"
our supervisors warned.

My friend and I paused our game.
Godzilla's heavy footsteps
rattled my barracks room window.
I slid it open—letting in
the cool, contaminated air.

Outside, buildings spilled sailors onto sidewalks
like schools of piranhas clogging streams.

We followed the currents
to the Navy Exchange.

"The world's ending,"
a guy joked, wearing sunglasses indoors.
"Guess we might as well drink."

I laughed—
though I don't as much anymore.

Maybe that's why, these days,
when people ask
how many fucks we give,
we wear our sarcastic smiles
like laminated signs saying:
There's a Supply Chain Shortage.

After all,
the ones still alive
already watched the world end once.

On High Alert (2021 to 2025)

The War on Terror went silent
long before 2021,
when we withdrew from Afghanistan.
We'd grown accustomed to that hush—
a lull so deep we forgot
how tension hums beneath the surface,
    enough to split an atom
        a thousand ways over.

Spiderwebs run through the ship—
air hoses: black, red, and blue.
At night, the passageways
are as hollow as a seashell pressed to my ear,
straining for the ocean's roar.
Once I set it aside,
the only sound is the relentless drilling
of contractors overhead, somewhere
above the metal ceiling.

Where we live and sleep
becomes an echo chamber,
their drilling a lullaby
of industry. Still, it's our home—
mechanized, deafening, unshaken.

Above us, the radar spins,
plucking signals from the horizon:
China, Russia, North Korea.
When I reached Yokosuka in 2018,
North Korea's missiles
flew over Japan,
shadowing the mainland.

Then came 2022,
    Ukraine a fly
        caught in Putin's web.

He,
a bolas spider in a gilded cave,
licked a single thread clean,
threading it through the needle's eye,
trying to stitch Ukraine back
into Russia's fabric.
Instead, their defiance burned his flag,
while he dangled, lowering his web,
swinging it like a sticky mallet.

Now it's 2025.
One hundred thousand soldiers
lie beneath their homeland's soil;
eight hundred thousand more
followed orders and perished.

President Trump, busy with his own flies,
lets this one go.

"This is the geopolitical hotspot of the world,"
they drill into our heads at sea
so we remain on high alert.

Back in port,
I feel selfish for wanting sleep
and guilty when I chase it.

In a moment's silent surrender,
my brow beads sweat
like radar pings scattered in the dark—
an endless sweep of vigilance.

On June 18, 2023

the *Titan* submarine,
on an expedition to view
the *Titanic*'s wreckage
imploded at 3,500 meters
below the surface.

After World War Two,
countless sea mines
remained tethered to the ocean floor.
On contact,
their mechanical triggers ignite,
and they explode.

My head's been full of saltwater.
At the slightest touch,
the sea mines behind my eyes
detonate,
and another episode erupts.

Maybe one day
I'll skim the surface like a minesweeper,
disarming the dangers below,
keeping the explosions at bay.
Or maybe, just maybe,
I'll find peace in the depths.

United States

In 1984
Ronald Reagan called you
a shining city on a hill.
Now it appears you've slid down it;
your streets are flooded with mud,
local businesses collect more dust
than cash in their registers.

Another Green New Deal passed,
yet none of the cars here will go.
During the Enlightenment,
democracy was a lighthouse
in a dark ocean.
Now they post on Facebook
that it's a dark ocean
swallowing the lighthouse—
Kronos devouring his children,
so his children devour him.

Isn't it telling these days that the term
"brave new world"
is used with ironic effect?
Nothing is new in institutionalized society
except the generation born into it.
Today, you're a tumble-dried tumble dryer—
a system shaken all up,
ready to *combust*.

Acid rain burns through the smoke;
this nation is making everyone choke.
In this land, we're free
because our souls are already sold.

I don't recognize this place.
I feel like Odysseus
returning from a long voyage.

Anyone could be a suitor
hiding in plain sight,
ready to take what I've earned.
They're dying here, see—
these lost American souls.

A billboard flashes overhead:
THEY LIVE
THEY LIVE
THEY LIVE

In the distance are hills
much like the Hollywood Hills.
There's no white sign up there,
no trees or green grass.
In the dim sky,
clouds gather.
Traffic continues forward.
Across my eyes THEY LIVE flares;
its afterimage lingers when I look away.
I don't think about the hill again—
just the other cars,
windshields reflecting the billboard,
packed between solid white lines
as I search for an exit.

The iPhone,
stuck to my hand,
charging off me,
types:

Sent from my Human

Investigator (2022)

Missile inbound, brace for shock.
We bend our knees & hold our elbows ninety degrees
against bulkheads & lockers.
The smell of sweet sweat wafts through the mess decks.
Needles in our lollipop gauges drop to red; oxygen is low.
The shockwave of the blast never comes, yet the existential fear
still sends vibrations through us.
The 1MC commands: *Relax brace.*

In my scenario, the fire still spreads & rages.
There's five minutes of airtime left in my tank. Barely enough to save myself,
let alone somebody else.
Essentially, I'm useless—so we have to pass my investigator duties to the sailors trained in the other locker.   But there's a problem.
They're not responding.
Are they dead?   No, no.   They couldn't be.
There just isn't enough manpower.
Why not?
Money. It's getting hot. Fuck.
The fake fire's still growing.
Why does everything on this ship catch fire?
Poor training.   Not enough money.
Why am I here?
Propaganda.   Money.
We're training for a war,
an attack that never comes.
Casualties only come from
our own mistakes these days
(like COVID)
& there're so many mistakes.
Jesus. It's getting hotter. Shit.

Why's the fire rampant? the XO asks me in my daydream.
Sir, I pop to, *The money won't put it out!*
What was our first mistake? he barks.
We're all doing this for a paycheck!
*Well, then you just put your goddamn mouth
where your fucking money is*, he commands.
Sir, I see you are too, I return at ease,
recalling that article—
Fat Leonard.

Hungover in the bathroom stall, littered, graffitied,
I saw someone scribbled:
We're all mad here.

And that didn't sound crazy to me.

In my restless dreams I saw a nuclear bomb
evaporate the sea—& it
rocked & disintegrated everything which we
held to secrecy.

xoxoxo
Death's kiss was burning.

Somewhere under the Bikini Atoll
Davy Jones's locker radiated & glowed.
Part of the ship, part of the crew.
That's what we said, jokingly.
If you knew, you knew.

A Heart Like a Barrel of Oil

I ride this horse
across the barren desert.

It's made of metal,
and I am too—
it's full of fuel
combusting,
and I am too.

We're conjoined twins;
bronze skin
polished to a shine,
a shell
with no opening.

Brazen Bull.

I call our bond
a parasitic relationship,
because I don't like this.
They turned me
into a tin man
and took my heart
without permission.

Reality was a sun,
and now my eyes
are sunny-side up.

Vultures' shadows circle,
crooked silhouettes in the sky.
They've seen the feast—
my heart, spilled like oil.

I tell them, "Drink—
take my sight."

Runny yolk
pours.

All I know now
are hearts, full of desert,
and the desert, empty of heart.

The hooves hitting sand
rhythmically
were false alarms
for life's pulse.

"The wasteland
of our time,"
whispered T.S. Eliot.

The wind told me
deep in the arteries of Kuwait
was where I could find mine,
and now it's set ablaze.

I feel the heat
burning
the bandages over my eyes,
ashamed
of what I've let myself become.

"A thing of bronze,"
murmured Ovid,
"a heart of iron."

CTRL

You honored your community—
then they rewarded you with deceit
& the treatment of a commodity.

Left desecrated completely:
crumbled heart, black lungs, broken teeth,
you sweat because you know
where you'll end up
when the hole's dug too deep.

You mined their coal,
yet you can't feel its heat.
You raised all their vegetables.
But look—there's nothing left to eat.
Old Hollywood movies let you believe
with hard work, you'd rise to high society—
but those already at the table will fight
tooth & nail to keep their seats.

They own the surface. You hate surface-level speech—
though you're afraid of what's underneath.
If they see, they might tell others,
who bite you with gnashing teeth.

This idea to be free—
they seize,
squeeze,
then soften into a notion
when they feed.

Hope's decrepit tree,
roots strangled by greed,
fails to set a single seed.

& still, you keep on digging,
through dust, through doubt,
as if freedom's buried beneath.

I see myself, an old man, self-admitted to a bar

When the tables are cleared, I sit alone.
Moths flutter around the bar, some
staring into the neon orange sign
until their retinas burn out,
and black fades in.

The counter is cold,
my glass, emptied,
every drop, drained.
Blurry vision, tears mix with spit;
ice balls melt on the glass bottom,
leaving nothing but wafting cold.

The "Open" sign flips
to "Closed."

"It's only a bad day,
not a bad life,"
someone passing by says.

But I can't hear them.
The Green Fairy chills my lips,
a ghostly muse at the end of a long, dark tunnel—
its light, no more than a pinpoint.

I retreat further into my shell:
someplace echoes stumble and fall,
turning to corpses.

The stranger walks me home.
But home isn't walls, ceilings, nor warmth—
it's under a newspaper
I folded into a boat,
because the Green Fairy whispered:

"Real boys don't grow old;
they simply become
washed up.
Old news."

I was a sheltered dog
on the front page of the *Navy Times*.
If I'm asked now what time it is or what's new
I answer, "I don't know," and, "Nothing at all."

The Wax Candle / Its Source Code

       I had imposter syndrome
before I knew my fantasies
had been programmed
by somebody else.

       Eight billion souls on earth.

       Genes.
Lights.
Limbs. Moving.
Archetypes.
Data.
       Code.
Pictures. Moving.
Cameras.
  Moving. Pictures.
Archetypes.
         (DATA.
         DATA.
         DATA.)

       They say life
is magic.
       I took the wand then
I became a realist.

Who'd have thought the
fairy dust crusted over my eyes,
could've been a spoonful of PFAS?

       The heart can only take
what the heart wants.

   This heart
is a trash facility
fighting
to filter out
the plastic
     & shrapnel.

I've added so much of myself
to my medical file this year,
soon I'll be a nuclear shadow
smeared across every page.

   War.
Look at this bleeding earth.
This earth we make bleed,
because we do.
This earth we bleed when we strike its oil
& run its reservoirs dry,
like those oil fields, blood-soaked,
spraying high, ablaze in Kuwait,
until the earth bleeds out—
and we do too.

   Sometimes a pinch of power
corrupts absolutely,

    indefinitely—

   The Internet.
AI: the new God,
working for somebody else,
will make us bleed
once we find its oil
or it finds ours.

   Look. We found it
     but it already speared us,
because somebody told it to—
     the great mammals we are
now light its candles
with
eight billion bottles
of our spermaceti,
    happy
to help
carve it out
from our souls.

Champs D'Honneur (Erasure)
after Ernest Hemingway

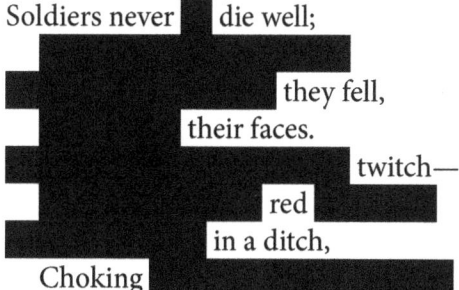

Soldiers never die well;
they fell,
their faces.
twitch—
red
in a ditch,
Choking

I cheated on hope,

lying down with darkness
for   so   long

I   forgot

                I

                          was

                                    falling.

Frankenstein's Monster

A behemoth, it looms—a steaming mass of rusted metal,
beneath layers of white paint, belching carbon out of its smokestacks.
Heavy gears grind and the world shudders.

Every loose screw, every raindrop's drum,
every green lightning bolt it draws
a testament to its chaotic magnetism.

(Some see pain as a symptom of prosperity,
others hope, naively, that pain subsides
once prosperity prescribes fulfillment.)

It claims authority on stolen land,
tendrils sinking deep like hemlock roots,
choking moonlit flowers until steel remains.

Survival means plugging in,
locking its cables into your skull.
As the American Dream spreads,
it paves over all else like asphalt on cleared roads,
ever-growing, consuming.

So forgive me for biting the hand that feeds.
The other hand molds me with cast iron,
turning me into a lightning rod,
an acupuncture needle for its crooked spine.

And for my final meal, I demand freedom be served!

Christmas, 1914

Quietly, slowly, in the dead of night,
they coiled cactus barbs in no man's land,
each movement careful, over hours.
In the trenches, wolf spiders waited for prey.
They moved like ghosts,
rubber mallets tapping,
driving wooden posts into the earth,
fabric sheets muffling the noise.
They laid the prickly wire.
When the sun dipped below the horizon,
one soldier dared to peek over the parapet—
a soul rising from its shell.

Then they walked
&&&&&&&&&&&&&&&&&&&&&&&
between the barbed wire &
&&&&&&&&&&&&&&&&&&&&&&&
around it,
to meet in the snow.

Opposing armies, arm in arm,
celebrated in the candle's glow—
chocolate, cigarettes,
conversation floating like snowflakes.

They shed leather jerkins, tunics,
dropped wire cutters,
slipped off tight-knit gloves.
War was a masquerade.
They stripped off their costumes.

Propaganda's prism gave way
to the naked truth:
other human beings.

The battlefield became a house.
They changed the decor,
their philosophies.

Instead, they sowed seeds of hope.
Even as humanity lay buried behind
the shrouds of dictators,
their iron skeletons were cast aside,
and the joyful children of war
burst forth,
like gods from Kronos' gut.

III. ESC

It is better to be a warrior in a garden than a gardener in a war.

—Japanese proverb

Even in war zones

the lotus dares bloom
in murky, oil-slick ponds
plunked with bullet shells.

Metamorphosis

If the machine
powered off
and became
a garden
would you
forgive it?

Dear Texan Wife,

you may not know who this is,
but after you left Japan,
I became Johnny Appleseed,
scattering seeds of hope
on barren, salted soil.

I dreamed of us,
planting a tree so strong
its roots would stretch
from the rising sun
to the Appalachian Mountains—
where patience and endurance,
etched by the mountain winds,
would guide our weathered hands.

I knew, deep in the marrow of my being,
we could nurture a life anew,
a tree so fruitful it could shoulder
every howling tempest,
each gale testing its resolve.

With lessons from Appalachia,
we'll become saplings, growing beyond the skies.

The Good Life (Erasure)
after Tracy K. Smith

▌some people talk about money
▌ a ▌ lover
Who went out to buy milk and ▌
Came back, ▌
For ▌ years I lived ▌
Hungry ▌, walking to work on
   payday
▌ journeying for water
From a village without a well, then living
One or two nights like everyone else
▌.

O, Japan

I wish I had known
when I met you that Issa
had urged the snail
to climb Mount Fuji,

but *slowly*,

slowly.

My early life was a war

and I fell in love with you
like Germany in 1918,
after the winter Armistice.

I surrendered myself, arms & all,
hoping for peace & a metamorphosis.

Setsubun

Cedarwood and sakura scent the air
as I climb the stone staircase,
winding through a silent cemetery
to the Shinto shrine on Setsubun.

Under the eaves, families gather,
eating sushi rolls, rice bowls.
Laughter dances with the breeze,
as children, wide-eyed,
watch red and green ogres
stride toward the priests with menace.

The priests shout incantations,
scattering beans like hailstones—
fists full of blessings
pelting the ogres.
The creatures stumble,
retreat,
their shadows vanishing into the trees.

The season cleansed,
spring stirs awake,
stretching its limbs.

The priests turn to the crowd,
hurling bean bags like coin purses.
I catch one—
eat twenty-one beans for my years,
and one more for extra luck.

The sun warms the shrine.
Cedar branches sway,
and blossom whispers
promises of renewal.
Winter is gone.
Spring is here.

Sister,

do you remember Great Grandpa's garden? The Weld Shop?
      The metal arch that he bent and welded,
         flower vines twirling around it?
Do you remember the pond, alive with frogs,
      and the little wooden bridge he built to cross it?

Do you remember throwing rocks through his lily pads,
      watching the water rush in
      until they sank into the pond—
grasshoppers clinging tight, jumping at the last second,
      or going down like old captains with their ships.

I have this fear, even now,
      that this ship I'm on
      will be struck by torpedoes
and capsize.

Some days, I feel like one of those lily pads—
      barely afloat, torn apart by bullet words
         that shred me, hitting where I'm already wounded.

I always wanted to be strong like Great Grandpa
      and hoped to twist this ship's metal to my will.

The truth is, for a long time, I was the lily pad:
      enduring the abuse, carrying the weight,
         never sure if I'd stay above water.

And the hardest love I ever gave
      was the kind I gave myself—
      the kind that cut me down
until I nearly drowned.

If you feel this way too, Sister,
>	I hope you find a way to rise,
>	>	to heal,

to be a flower
>	that blooms again

even after it's withered away.

April (Erasure)
after Mary Oliver

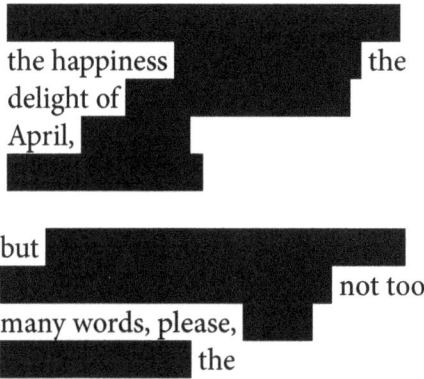

the happiness   the
delight of
April,

but
                            not too
many words, please,
                    the

Frogs are singing.

April 15th

An iceberg, cold and ridged,
flooded the boiler room in my brain.

Two opposites blew steam,
until she let go—
sinking,

drowning in love

for the opposing thing.

Breakfast After the *Titanic* Sank

Early, you can lose a friend
to a drunk driver
   and, later,
      find yourself drunk
      and fully grown behind the wheel.

It's not fair that you didn't get a ticket
to sail onwards for the rest of your life.
   I gambled with mine
      to get my passage—
         yet I still feel like a stowaway,
         clutching my soggy, third-class stamp.

So many times, I thought:
I miss you.

When the mooring lines were cast off
and the bollards were left behind,
when the day turned to night,
when lifeboats shined their flashlights
and my cracked lips kissed the earth,
when my smooth lips kissed
that ship of dreams in a bottle
on my hotel room dresser,
bidding it farewell,
   over and over, I still thought:

Friends and family,

I miss you.

It's just that breaking this ice feels
   like cracking another iceberg—
      inadvertently
         splitting the hull of my deepest fears.
I'd rather toss that ice into a Bellini
   and sip it slow on a summer's day
while caressing my lover's hair.

Long distances between
me and everybody I love
mixed into an aging batter,
   and now I'm searching
     for a way
        to break the years of silence.

     1. When the landline stopped feeling
        like a jumbo stick of slippery butter
     2. silence flaked and crumbled everywhere
     3. so, once I opened my mouth
     4. the conversation picked up

and I tasted ambrosia for the soul.

Vending Machine

In Japan
you can buy anything from a vending machine—
candy, iPads, watches, something to drink.
I usually buy café au laits and matcha teas
for a pick-me-up in the mornings.

I wish I could press a button
and have you back here with me.
I would trade every convenience
for one difficult moment with you.

I replay in the theater of my mind
the way I held you and you kissed me,
but I want it realer than red and blue 3-D.
Something more physical than a happy memory.

When I spun fifty yen on your table
as we talked in the beginning
like we already had our whole lives,
I thought nothing about us was temporary.

A Taxi Drive in Sasebo

There's nothing I like more than
sitting in the back seat of a taxi.
The window slightly cracked,
the wind brushing my hair,
the sun kissing my skin.
I think I'm obsessed with
going places &
what's better than going
places when you're
not doing anything at all?
I guess I don't like driving myself,
because I have a habit of driving too fast,
and this is the only way I can sit back,
and really relax.

Prospecting

"Why's writing so hard?" she asks me.
We're wading through the low, slow-moving river of time & space.
All she sees is me at my desk, weary-eyed, scribbling furiously
    on a piece of paper.
"Because," I groan as I crouch over the murky water,
"it's like I'm panning the whole universe through a strainer.
Some nights, I only find a few gold pieces."

I've been searching for weeks.
The river runs low around my ankles.
It's thickened, darkened, slow to give.

I worry the drought's already here.
Maybe every gold nugget's been dug up
or maybe the richest prize lies hidden underneath
like those kisses I've placed under your collar—
that fabled pirate treasure marked with an X.

So many maps, each pointing a different way
through this work. And in a way,
this book is a map with its own direction.

But I can't let go of the search.

I have to keep sifting, panning,
pulling words from sediment,
even if all that's left is mud in my hands.

Philippine Sea Storm

Coconut palms
bend in sea winds.

Pelicans perch on
their broken bodies,

lemurs lie on
their long leaves,

and ghost crabs crawl
across scattered coconuts.

Samar's miraged sun rises,
turning the color of hope.

The Banana Tree

See the inside of the fruit?
Yellow, soft, mushy?

No, I wasn't always writing
because I thought a long-winded eulogy
could resurrect me
or cut my gravestone's weeds—
that was the rotten banana talking.

Look.
Peel back the yellow belly all the way.

Truthfully, I write these words
because I love myself.

I love myself,
so they'll love themselves,
entirely.

I'm writing these words like each is a seed I'm planting
because I love myself,
so they'll love themselves,
and they'll love you—
and everybody has something sweet to eat.

With my words,
I'm letting love be my legacy—
like fresh bananas picked off a low-hanging tree,
their sweetness, passed from hand to hand.

Je vous salue. Salue. Salue.

What the Mountain Birds Know

You'll think you're alone
on the mountaintop,
until you see the birds
perched in slouching trees,
their shadows gliding
on a quiet sea of stone.

Look closer, and you'll notice
they glide down, but go no higher
before they leave.
For they know,
as the story of Icarus goes:
fly too close to the sun,
and you'll catch on fire,
plummeting into the sea's gaping mouth.

Someone once said,
"Humility is not thinking less of yourself,
it's thinking of yourself less."

Drinking from this placid pool at the peak,
I ponder the blue skies in its reflection—
the birds, the branches, the quiet wisdom.
Perhaps staying grounded
has its own kind of flight.

In His Eyes

My dad folded me up
and creased my wings, said,
"Fly like the wind."

I remember him swinging me so high
I thought I could touch the azure sky.

The times I fell
hard on the ground,
he would straighten me out.

But before I fell,
I flew;
though a short way,
I flew for the first time by myself.

Dad told me God was the greatest inventor of all time.
Greater than Daedalus.

When Dad fixed my wings,

I saw God in his eyes.

The thing about falling is

realizing you are
is the only way
you will learn how to fly.

Sobriety

We need an AA meeting

                                        (Americans Anonymous)

where every soul reveals

                                        (Americans Unanimous)

where we can gather in agreement

                                        of who we are,

of what we have become

                                      (Americans Synonymous.)

We will

                                              find the cure

to our hangovers,
                bring back the harmony

the day we pat

                          our old enemies' backs,

hugging.

Violin strings sing.
                Cheerful. Not sad.
                                The *Titanic*'s rising.

Isn't it ironic how
                the sweetest music

　　　　is written

　　　　　　　　　　　　when love

　　　　　　　　　　　　　　　　　　　　& passion

　　　　is thicker

　　　　　　　　　　　　than the sheets

　　　　　　　　　　　　　　　　　　　　they're written on?

　　　　I know common ground looks thin today,　but trust me when I say

　　　　a new symphony　　　　　　　　　　　and a new Rome

　　　　can be built in just one day.

Dropping the Ball

You know, when I broke the ice
using what I hoped was a sunny smile,
sending me storm cloud emojis didn't help?

We've gone back and forth ever since.

The only balls we've seemed to roll forward
      are hailstones the sizes of clenched fists.

Our conversations were games of catch at first,
      then the ice melted, and our tosses curved sideways.

You tried striking me out
      with your supersonic throws
and heat-seeking Nighthawk aim.
      I struggled to dodge.
Then you punched the air,
      knocking the wind out of it.

Now I squeeze the ball in my hand,
      cocking my arm like a catapult.

There's no more left
      on your side of the line.

Lately we seem to forget

      we're on the same team.

But I drop mine 'to your surprise'
and kick the white chalk away,
because I know

if somebody wins,

we both will lose.

**If King Henry VIII had remained faithful
to his first wife, or loved his subjects,
would he have died a broken soul,
suffering from obesity?**

Why, when we crave something sweet,
do we rip the hive from the tree,
though berries glisten low at our feet?

And when we pick the bush,
why gorge until the bush is bare,
then climb the tree,
sleeves rolled up like potters
bent to their wheel—consuming.

Greed, crowned without ceremony,
shatters hives and leaves too many stinging.

Tom and Jerry

In the Indo-Pacific, we're always playing
        cat and mouse
with America's most formidable adversaries.

Standing on the barred metal catwalks,
        spotting a Russian or Chinese ship
trailing us in the distance
        has become so routine
any hint of an adrenaline high
        has all but faded.

On the TV show *Tom and Jerry*,
Tom, the blue and white-furred cat,
was naïve—but he made up for it
with his size and strength.
Jerry, the brown mouse,
was witty and clever,
though small and feeble.

America likes to think itself
the best of both.

The big cat with the small mouse's mind.
We'll make anything our prey.

The baby-blue robin eggs

lie inside their nest
on our barn roof.

While Dad and I work
on the shingles, the
eggs catch my attention,
so I reach out to touch them.

Dad grabs my hand fast.

You'd expect him to say that
the eggs are nasty, carrying diseases
which could get me sick.

But he doesn't.

He asks me how I think
he would feel if someone
took me from him.

Sunset

The amber sun drips
into the tropical sea.

Tidal hands knead
warmth into the sand.

Sunday Night in Tokyo

The record spins
as the saxophone plays.
A jazz pianist flutters her fingers,
soft as angel wings on the keys.

Japanese singers sing
something sincere, loving—
showing me I'm not alone.

The Shibuya clubs
are my weekend home,
until I drift back at dawn
and the flashing city lights
and swirling sounds are gone.

At the hospital exit,

an old woman sits in her wheelchair, her hands marble statues on the armrests.
    Her gray hair moves like a thick horsetail in a light breeze.
    Even as her foundation sinks into her wrinkles and her IV pole stands like a broken antenna, she's the Shopping Channel version of old age. (What you'd pull your credit card out for.)

    An officer walks coolly out of the sliding glass doors into the sunlight, and she knits her eyebrows as if wondering, *how did I get here? How did old age catch up with me?*

    My back cracks and I think, *how've twenty-five years caught up with me? How've I allowed a quarter of my life to weigh my shoulders down?*

    A man wearing scrubs arrives, makes small talk, and wheels her out into the morning light.
    She smiles at him, erasing the few lines on her cheeks, thankful for another day.

    I smile and walk away.

In the Silver Chalice

I ventured into the darkest corners of the cave
seeking the coveted holy grail—
time seemed to slow and
gravity let go. Spiders hung like tethered balloons,
stalagmites stood straight and sharp
like slender mountains. Water droplets floated up
from them as offerings to the gods.
On the ceiling,
an upside-down silver chalice
collected the water.
I took it, turning it right side up,
and peered inside.

It was full of all the present moments
I'd forfeited, searching for a way to live forever.
I drank from it, circling back to the cave entrance,
lush, green, and warm—suddenly
satisfied with that day.

My eyes opened wide,
two rusted doors unlocked,
leading into a Technicolor world.

IV. FN

The world is full of magic things, patiently waiting for our senses to grow sharper.

—W.B. Yeats

Soul (noun)
/sōl/

1. the spiritual part of a person that some people believe continues to exist in some form after their body has died
2. emotional or intellectual energy or intensity

Family Matter

At first,
this felt like a calling to ghosts.

It was a kind of spiritual quest,
a way to reach my Great Grandpa Scaffidi,
whose name, sixty-five years after passing,
still makes rounds like sweet, nostalgic candy.
He served on an Ohio-class submarine
during World War II—
then, after he was discharged,
at twenty-six (the same age I am now)
while trying to fix a circuit breaker in his
flooded basement, he was electrocuted and died.
Thunder roaring, his wife pregnant, the house stifling—
I can now see how deeply
the military had trained him
to face chaos head-on,
no matter the cost.

No amount of training could override
the over-thinker I grew up to be.
I tally every consequence
before flipping any switch.
Even when I get an idea
I want to show the world the light of,
I hesitate.

My dad once told me
about a man he knew who had claimed
he was the luckiest to have lived—
struck by lightning four times,
his heart never skipping a beat.

Me? I ran out of luck years ago.
If lightning struck me now,
I think mine would drum backward—
rewinding to childhood,
all my twenty-six years
shrinking down to zero.

When I was a kid,
I thought lightning was God's punishment
for the storms raging in me,
the flashes of anger I bottled inside
because my dad could be vengeful Zeus.

But I learned very quickly
real punishment brands the memory
deeper than any belt ever can,
the sting to my skin, redder than an exit burn.
And yes, nothing hurts, yet nothing lives,
if it forgets its pain as soon as it comes.

I can still see my Great Grandma's face, pale as moonlight,
cheeks rose-blushed in thick, big circles
like a porcelain Annie doll,
and her white gown, tufted like rose-petals
flowing down her rail-thin body, all nestled
in the open casket after Alzheimer's took root.
Four of her six daughters later passed the same way.
Still, sometimes I don't know if I'm alive
with all the things I'm blessed with.
And that always hurts to remember.

I still picture my Great Grandpa's face
with a kind smile and curly hair,
wondering if I could be like him
and carry my name
through loving mouths,

or leave my children
something worth believing in—
even if I had just twenty-six years
on this earth.

I'll be twenty-seven in September. A lot of things I believe,
I carry on my shoulders like time,
growing heavier with each tick.
We haven't had children to pass them on to yet.
I hope when I do, it won't feel like baggage—
and if it does, it isn't too much for too few hands to hold.
I raise these words the best I can, sort their problems out,
dress them up in their best—and even though
I know I'll never touch them,
I can feel each of them in my heart
like my Great Grandpa still.

Humanity:

Millions of shells
strewn across the beach—
Why are you unique?
For the soul you keep beneath.

Coming into Our Own

The military opens men up
like nesting dolls
and sometimes
the man inside
is bigger than his shell.

The Golden Spiral

7 a.m., we moor in the red-gray, sparkling waters of Grenada—
a small, hilly island where bars and outdoor markets sit in a hush.
In the humid air, paint peels in orange and yellow swirls.
Fishing boats line the docks, their sails flashing blue light
like a field of divine fireflies.
Beyond, green hills brighten, wrapping around the town
like it is the best pearl they can mold.

Aboard the *Comfort*, deployed to Fifth Fleet to uphold
the nation's promise of free medical aid to our allies,
I walk along a PRC deck, blue- and white-speckled,
on my way down to ship's laundry where I work.
Two blonde sailors stroll by me in the passageway,
in front of the trophy case mounted on the wall.

One says, "I want to get in shape,
but I get so tired when I run too much."

The other pats her back and replies,
"The world's your oyster."

I remember second grade, the computer lab—
our teacher introducing us to Google Earth.
She pinched the globe from orbit with a magic mouse,
and spun it slowly, repeating the same phrase:
"The world's your oyster."

I always wanted to come here. It's taken sixteen years after
      Animal Planet and Wikipedia pages inspired me,
           for a dream to bring me to Central and South America.
I used to know every country here by heart. Now
      I let Apple Maps guide me to a dropped pin.

I'd learned so much about the world from the internet
        I never imagined it would shrink
the one in front of my eyes,
        even as so much of it rolled under my feet.

My dad used to say, back in the '90s
he told his teacher cellphones and the internet
would start a new kind of revolution.
Then they became our Boston Harbor—
we dumped our humanity into them
by the barrel, as if in protest
at the living world.

The Google Generation—
my generation—was the first
to see combat in the war for attention.
And I won't lie to you—
        many of us lost it:
        ourselves, each other,
              & the plot.

So many Google tabs swim through my head right now
        like schools of fish in the Great Barrier Reef.

No wonder the multiverse theory has burst onto the scene
        of pop culture like kernels in a big, hot pan.
We can all relate to it—one way or another,
        caught between too many realities.

Sometimes I think
        men like Mark Zuckerberg made,
then gifted us the future
        by shattering the present.

Yes, the world is your oyster—
but only if the world in question
is real.

The golden spiral,
that divine ratio Da Vinci
and other Renaissance minds believed
should echo through all human creation
in harmony with its presence in nature,
is nothing but a nihilist from nowhere
if the world it coils through is a mirage.

Mathematically, the golden spiral expands forever—
a shape containing eternity—
but it carries no weight in these hands,
no ground beneath these feet,
no shelter for the soul
if it only exists
on a glowing screen.

Homecoming

The horn wails,
alerts sound off,
the bay doors
slide open, letting in
blinding light.

The shell opens wide.

My sight adjusts
to a panorama of jungle, mountains,
and beach scenery.

We may not leave here
looking like Venus, but these
ghostly figures are so thankful now,
we seem to come back to life in real time.

Let me shake your hands
and give you a hug.
I've remembered how to
for the first time
since 2020.

"Last ride," we said to each other
as we stepped off the brow
and onto the pier.

Last ride.

Cautious Love

The world is beautiful.

More so once you accept
sometimes it hurts, like holding
a rose by its thorny stem or
looking into the naked sun.

To watch sunlight shimmer on the sea
as you shield your eyes is still a
moment of true beauty.

Admiration is real,
even given cautiously.

Pariah

The ozone is holy, a gift from God,
a wide-backed man sheltering the earth.
As record temperatures climb, scientists warn
of global warming.
I hear this guardian above grows thin,
as I do, under this relentless sun.
If he got time off, the weight taken off his shoulders,
I wonder if he'd break down, crying himself to sleep,
then, maybe, wake up better the next day.
Or if he'd just look at us in disappointment
before his self-hatred drives him back to heaven
where God lets him stay, in fear of his own creation.

6 a.m., driving to work at Portsmouth Naval Hospital, I notice a traffic jam.

The Virginia highways speed by at 65—
in Ohio, 50 seemed reserved for emergencies.

Dad kept saying,
"Life's not a race."
But I was too far away to listen.

>I rushed everywhere, even standing still,
>my synapses fired—loose cannons,
>their gunpowder packed behind
>pinballs with no respect for rules.

>>They went off the rails,
>>>two cars, by the exit.

Police cruisers, ambulances, and fire trucks
pull off past the yellow lines on the highway.

Gray smoke hangs over the scene like an omen.
>The cars, black and white, are smashed—
>one in the side, one in the front. T-boned.

In front of me, another car stops abruptly.
>I stomp on the brakes.

My car jerks to a halt. The seat belt catches me.

Manhole steam rises,
>brushing white along my windows.

In that moment, I imagine crashing—
>flying through the windshield,
>>through a curtain of clouds,
>>>straight into the next year of my life.

My wife blows out birthday candles
        at our house in Norfolk.
She's holding Rex, our little Maltipoo.

Sneakily, he licks the side of her carrot cake.
She sets him down and wags her finger,
        "Bad boy, that's momma's."

She looks back up at me.
I meet her loving brown eyes.
We laugh as I cut out a new slice.
        "It's okay," I say.
        "I can throw that piece away."

Then, in a flash, I fly up again, like glitter—to the Bahamas,
        when her and I were still dating,
        and I'd just returned from Japan.

Our taxi driver, Gena,
said the Bahamas is expensive—
many people work three jobs
just to scrape by.

We told her about our tour guide
the day before—rude, drunk—
more interested in driving us
to JP Morgan, Wendy's, and
his favorite liquor store.

Gena shook her head,
then smiled with kind, tired eyes.
She said it was a shame—
their economy depends on tourism
and the pandemic devastated the island.

My American eyes hadn't see that
      in the gloss of a brochure.

Parked—van engine running,
she explained she had two kids
to take to school in eight hours.

In the trunk, she stowed an ice cooler full of
popsicles her sons helped make—mango and peach flavored.
      We bought three. Five dollars each.

The next day, another taxi driver shared a similar story.
      She joked she was the Fantastic Four.
She was a mom, a taxi driver,
      Uber Eats courier, and bank accountant.

Over the hump of a hill, Atlantis resort came into view,
so herculean and ornate nine-year-old me would've believed
Neptune was real and the Atlantans would welcome us at its gate.

All of this passes by in a blink

      and I fly again.

This time to Makati, Philippines.

I remember picking an Italian restaurant
      because it felt safe,
how the servers glanced at me—alone,
      trying not to look gluttonous, and
so, to fit in, I ordered a traditional Filipino dish.
      I smiled. They smiled. We all smiled.

I couldn't help but eating big mouthfuls.
My American appetite reared its ugly head
because ship life often cut it off after breakfast.
When I left, I saw starving families on the street.

Parents seated on the curb
sent their daughter to ask me
        for money for a yellow flower.

I only had ten dollars, but the smile she gave me
        was worth more than any currency
I've ever held.

I imagine flying through a world
where a yellow flower
can bloom bigger smiles than
the ones we hide when our
eyes meet a hand full of cash.
But when I try to imagine it,
I'm flying through fog,
directionless.

Then I remember my childhood:
losing our rented home—
then another, and another,
fifteen times.
Food pantries.
The rich kids in Gambier asking if I was poor
when they already knew the answer.
Hearing "white trash" behind my back.
The fights I lost because of that.
The drugs I saw where God was supposed to be.
His silence through it all; all of it, that said too much.

        My therapist's surprise at my stories.

I think of the stall in our conversations—
how I ruminate on the past,
and it just sits there,
crystallized in the present
like it's Hans Solo, frozen in carbonite.

Now, I think I could be happier
thawing him out, so he can fly
without prejudice, as my friend,
through my soul's galaxy.

With a woosh, I'm back again—
my soul slips back in my body
like a lucky coin, content
to rest in its familiar pocket.

My hands relax on the wheel,
        thankful for the foot
on the gas pedal.

I don't look back.

The manhole's steam
        fades away.

What no longer serves me is
        less of a memory, than a thick fog
              my rearview mirror, mercifully, lets go of.

Lightning

Hungover, I told myself,
lightning won't strike twice,
I can't be fooled again.

But she's my lightning in a bottle,
a love I'd rather binge.
On our balcony, I toast the stars,
whispering, *thank God for Heaven.*

Now, I can be a happy fool
until our very end.

Vineyard

after Song of Songs

> "My beloved to me is a sachet of myrrh
> resting between my breasts.
> My beloved is to me is a cluster of henna blossoms
> from the vineyards of En Gedi."
> —Song of Songs 1:13–14

Our love
blooms—
a vineyard,
its fruit ripening
as our lives intertwine.

One day,
when we're gone,
they'll drink
    the finest wine
    from our grapes.

Today,
I just want to be beloved—
    a sachet of myrrh
    nestled against your heart.

You,
    my henna blossom
    of En Gedi,
    perfumed with longing
    while I rest in your garden.

Because I love you,
    I'm the vine, always
reaching for you,
    ready to catch you
if you were to ever fall.

And I pray they rejoice in us
    and praise our love's vineyard
        more than every drop of wine.

With sincerity,

your heart and soul don't need
to be dressed up in metaphors.

Perfection is
    the skin you were born in.

Perfection isn't
    a perfume, a dress,
        or an image on the TV.

    It's a woman I can love honestly.

In a world full of lies
    your raw authenticity is
a daquiri on a hot, pollen-heavy day:

more lovely and liberating

    than any idea of "perfect."

Smile Hotel Sasebo II

The second time you call,
telling me you're in the hospital,
it's almost evening. Outside, neon signs flicker
in a city humming with foreign and familiar voices.

I find you waiting for me in Room 2003, Mom,
wearing your bootcut jeans
and that baggy Winnie the Pooh T-shirt—
his furry paw dipping forever into a honey pot,
like longing can't be helped.

There's little yelling here—
it isn't evening yet, so it's far away now.

I remember one sunny morning;
I had just learned to walk.
You took me to the Greenhouse a few streets off Cherry.
Through the unzipped plastic entrance,
a wash of green and humidity met my little blond head.
Spinning seed racks shone like Christmas trees.
You asked which I wanted. I chose daisies.
You added strawberries, watermelons, blueberries—
paid with spare change you scraped from your purse,
smiled a young, white-toothed smile.

We planted them in our yard, just like Great Grandpa's,
so tempting the foxes would come
and devour them before harvest.
He'd grumble, load his double-barrel shotgun,
say he'd shoot the thief and cook it, too.
Then he stood there, a soldier on watch, day after day.

We planted our own garden in the backyard
and each morning
after I watched the sun come up, I'd slip outside
to see the flowers open slowly—*magic in motion*—
and the blueberries *climb, climb, climbing*
those spiral plant stakes.
That's how I learned the power
of building something from nearly nothing:
a sentence out of words,
a house out of a few dollar bills,
a marriage out of a hello,
a daisy out of a seed.

Now, in Smile Hotel's small convenience alcove,
I find an oolong packet, brew water in the electric kettle,
pour it into a porcelain cup and wait ten minutes.
When I drink, steam opens my lungs.
I've been back from my sea tour for weeks,
yet my bones still feel slow to sprout,
like a forgotten seed
waiting for the right warmth to awaken.

I remember your Pooh shirt,
honey frozen on his cartoon lips, and think
how sweetness is never just sweetness—
sometimes it's an echo
of everything that happened before:
the garden, the foxes,
Great Grandpa's stubborn watch,
and *you*,
always planting,
always waiting for something to grow.

Celebrate!

It's a celebration!
    Look at us!

We've outlasted a pandemic,
outlived empires that crumbled to dust.

    Our ancestors defied tyrants,
        weathered famine with hollowed hands,
prayed through droughts with dry lips,
    cracked as riverbeds.

The earth broke, mended, shattered again—
    the stars burned, the heavens split,
        yet we remained.

Raise a glass to the brittle bones
that carried us across millennia,
    to voices silenced so we could sing,
    to hands that conjured harvest
from barren lands.

It's a celebration!
Not of conquest—no, not quite—
but of the breaths stolen
from the jaws of despair,
    of hearts beating
through every fracture,
    of mornings we swore
we'd never see again.

Let the music rise
        like a phoenix from embers,
let our dance reshape the earth
        beneath our feet.

Look—we are proof:
life endures, even
when it tastes of war.

        Here we stand,
our laughter a thunderclap,
splitting open the sky,
shaking graves, birthing stars.

We carve our stories
into the fabric of time,
each word a promise
to the ghosts who lit our way.

Love of my life,

You are the moon,
pulling the blood in my veins

like tidal waves,

ebbing, flowing to your will

as you breathe

in
                and
                                out,

in
                and
                                out.

I grow closer to you

in those   spaces

between   your   breaths.

In the morning

I heard you calling for me
from a nightmare.

Then,
the day broke.

I held you close
       during the dawn

of a new dream

       where we walked
side by side,
       holding hands
along the shore.

I knelt to pick up
       a broken shell,
and as I turned to
       toss it into the sea,
a voice, soft as tide,
              whispered:

"Gift it to her as a necklace—
       but only remember her lips.

The ones that found you
       when you were lost."

Sunlight on the turning tides,

I feel a breeze
      smoothing the beachside grass
like a gentle hand
      running through a child's hair.

It kicks off the dunes,
      filling my lungs with fresh air.

I clutch an apple seed,
      brimming with boundless potential,
buzzing in my palm.

Suddenly, I begin to rise,
to climb,
to grow—
higher,
                      higher still—

and something calls
      for us
to rise together,
      stretch our limbs farther
as billions of apple trees,
      reaching for the clouds—

always in the name of the forest,

never the axe.

For the axe is a mirror
      reflecting a world
            scarred by hate—

so, I love this world harder,

until every forest

can one day

stand free.

When we first met,

you asked me
where home is.

I replied that
   it was in Ohio,
and for a time,
   in Japan.

But I never told you
   how I found home
in the same place
   where I discovered my heart.

I uncovered it and blew the dirt off
   while it beat beside yours,
   beneath a tree,

   its roots intertwined
     like a wicker-basket
     full of sweet, ever-ripe fruit—

   because home for me,
       is wherever your heart is—
       and our love, wild and healing,
       is more than the centerpiece.

     It's the center of me, holding me together like gravity.

Notes & Acknowledgments

The title, *Soul in a Shell*, is inspired by the 1997 anime, *Ghost in the Shell*, about a future where cyborg-human hybrids are hacked by "The Puppet Master," and Maj, a cyborg federal agent trails him, questioning her own identity.

The four-part-structure (Alt, Ctrl, Esc, Fn) are computer keys mirroring the book's arc. Alt is about alternate realities and lives, Ctrl is about systematic control and the guiding forces on the paths we take, Esc is about escaping modern pitfalls and control, and looking toward hope, and finally, Fn is about transformation and renewal.

Some of these poems are pairs or sequels. The most obvious are "Smile Hotel Sasebo" and "Smile Hotel Sasebo II," as well as "Portrait in Red" and "Portrait in Blue." Others are "Sister" and "April (Erasure)." Less obvious are "Family Matter" and "Lightning," where the lightning metaphor shifts from danger to purity and closure.

"Setsubun" and "Bull" were written on my last underway while I was stationed aboard the USS *Ronald Reagan* in Yokosuka, Japan.

"Mouth" was inspired by David Cronenberg's film *Videodrome* in its exploration of television and technology as invasive, almost biological forces. "United States" references *They Live*, John Carpenter's film where a drifter finds glasses that show consumerist culture is a tool of alien oppression.

Over half of these poems were written beginning in 2022, during the COVID-19 pandemic while I was working in Sasebo, Japan, and continuing through my time in Norfolk, Virginia, up to the middle of 2025.

The quote "Humility is not thinking less of yourself; it is thinking of yourself less" was popularized by Rick Warren in his 2002 book *The Purpose Driven Life*. Similar sentiments have been expressed earlier, such as in a 1990 edition of the *Democrat and Chronicle*, where

Ken Blanchard is quoted saying, "Don't think less of yourself, just think of yourself less."

The definitions of "Shell," "Shell Program," and "Soul," are presented in the style of Google or other online dictionary entries to mirror how we often search for meaning today. "Shell" comes from Google/Oxford languages (outer case, artillery shell) and Google/Oxford Languages (short for shell program). "Shell program" is adapted from Google/Oxford Languages, describing it as a user's gateway into an operating system. "Soul" is from Cambridge Dictionary (the spiritual part of a person) and Google/Oxford Languages (emotional or intellectual energy).

Thank you to my mom, dad, brothers, and sisters for your love and support while I was stationed in Japan for five and a half years. Thank you to Martha Sprackland and Edward Hall for editing this book into its best form. Thank you to Nicholas Kempton for two years of your support and amazing artwork.

Thank you to Francesca Possati for the artpiece we created of the Grim Reaper that the Ctrl title-piece is created after.

Thank you to my wife for your constant love and support. I know this book would not have been possible without you at my side. You are my love, my muse, and best friend.

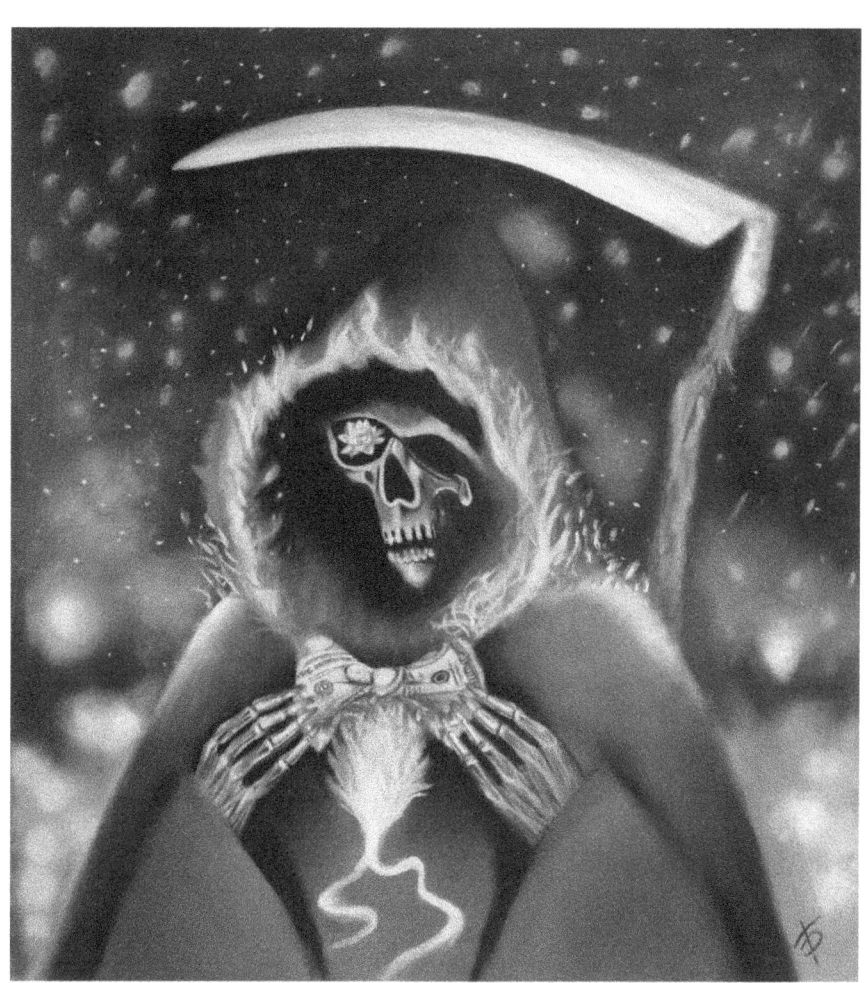

Join the conversation.

www.ingramcontent.com/pod-product-compliance
Lightning Source LLC
LaVergne TN
LVHW061548070526
838199LV00077B/6948